# I Ain't Going to College!

# Decision-Making Guide for Life After High School

By

Marlo L. Prioleau

## Dedication

I was raised by a village. My parents, step-parents, sisters, aunts, uncles, close relatives and neighborhood friends all played a role in my development. I dedicate this book to my grandmother, Carrie M. Prioleau, for consistently being a positive force in my life. Always there, always honest, always giving even when there was not much to give. The core of who I am is because of you.

# Table of Contents

# Introduction

Learning never stops, but it certainly has a starting point, which is different for everyone. I am not talking about textbook learning; I am talking about the intangible learning that takes you from ordinary to extraordinary. This type of learning changes who you are and it takes place at different times in your life. During my senior year of high school, I thought I had reached the highest level of learning I could reach. I didn't think I had anything else to learn. It was not until my 13th year of school, which was my first year of college at South Carolina State University that I realized everything I thought I knew about myself was about to change, mostly due to my new environment. I wrote this book to help young people understand that nothing is more important than learning all that you can and formally educating yourself. Whether you learn a trade and obtain a two year degree or move on to a four year college or university, or join the armed forces upon graduating from high school you, absolutely need a game plan for life after high school. When the storms of life begin to rage, and the road gets tough my education is one of the constant factors in my life that keeps me safe, sheltered and financially able to keep moving forward. Knowing that I was able to start and finish something so challenging and so rewarding still moves me to this day. Below are a few short stories that I hope will inspire you to one day live out your dream and achieve great success that is not only measured by money and rewarding careers, but also measured by happiness, stability, and a feeling of accomplishment because you have taken the time to educate yourself beyond high school.

# Chapter 1

# College What's The Point?

Why should I go to college? What is the point? If I had one dollar for the number of times I have answered this question, I would certainly not be writing this book. I would be lying on the beach dictating these words and someone else would be doing all the work- typing it up for me because I would be rich! Nonetheless, my answer is very simple, but there are multiple answers! Come on now; you didn't think I was going to give you the short answer now, did you? College will allow you to receive an education which will set you apart from others and ultimately lead you down a path of success if you take full advantage of its resources while you are there. It's a requirement to gain access to better information so one can be professionally groomed for the right opportunity and then seize it! Simply by going to class daily you will learn new things and start to evolve as a person due to being in this new environment. If you exert the effort and study hard, you will position yourself for success based on the major you have chosen. Now that's my textbook answer which is all true but lean in closely....let me tell you the REAL answer. Ultimately, attending college is about preparing for a career, and it shows employers one thing. It tells whether you have the ability to start a task and finish it. Graduating with a college degree is one of the hardest things a person will accomplish in life. If it was easy everyone would have a college degree. All of your friends would follow the traditional path of graduating from high school, moving on to college and starting a great job, right? So why is the ability to finish something such a big deal? As you move through life, the opportunity to start tasks will occur frequently. You will start many different projects and tasks all the time. Many will start writing a song or book, but they will not finish, many will start selling sneakers, hats, designing t-shirts, creating video games but they will not finish it. Many students will start high school every year all across America yet; many will not finish. Many will start college and also fall short of the goal which is to do what? FINISH. Completing the task shows not only employers, but it shows the whole world that you can do exactly what you set out to do. College is full of ups and downs, highs and lows, everything from understanding how to manage your time so you can get all of your homework and assignments done, to figuring out how to manage your money, and relationships, to paying bills and being responsible as you grow into a young adult. Doing all these things successfully allow you to do one thing, graduate with the college degree of your choice. It's a clear signal that you know how to make decisions, think critically, overcome obstacles, work hard, handle many tasks at once, meet deadlines, interact socially, communicate, and work with others. The degree itself will serve as a stamp of approval based on a standard of unwritten rules that cannot be asked about during a job interview. A college degree will allow you to be evenly matched against your peers who have also prepared themselves and is the general gateway to having a career versus having a job. Many other variables will play into this but if you can get to the finish line, and really think about some of the topics discussed in this book you will be able to show the world that you are not a person who starts things and doesn't finish them, but instead a polished college graduate ready to take on the world. Most importantly, graduating and finishing a college degree proves to one person, the most important person you will ever meet, sometimes your toughest critic, other times your biggest cheerleader, YOU, that anything is possible if only you stay the course.

### *#Minutewithmarlo: Decision*

### Importance of Education and Finishing Task

1.  Why is going to college so important?

2.  Why is it important to complete a task once you have    started it?

3.  Are there any unfinished tasks in your life that you need to complete? List them below and think about how you can tackle them one by one.

# Chapter 2

# The Beginning

I was coming of age during the 1980's, which was around the time President Ronald Reagan declared and made popular the "War on Drugs". This was a dangerous time not only in Sumter, but all across America because this is when crack cocaine was tearing through the black community in particular. My two sisters and I lived with my mother's parents. My Grandfather was Samuel (Daddy-O) as we called him and Elizabeth or Grandma as we referred to her. We grew up very poor and certainly saw our fair share of tough times. We would argue often about many things, but one thing was always a hot topic, the phone. Over the years there were many times that I needed to use the phone. Something so simple often came with backlash. "Daddy-O," I said, in a stern voice. I need to use the phone to call my daddy. He started laughing hysterically. "Your daddy doesn't want to talk to you, why would you bother him?" He does too, I said. He told me to call him when I needed something, and I need to call him, I explained No, he said, "Calling him cost me money" and just like that there would be no phone call for me on this day. I knew the only thing I could do was to wait until he goes to work in the morning, sneak into his room and use the phone. That morning my grandma Liz left the house early to go to the grocery store. I opened the bedroom door and found the room ice cold. An air conditioner was in the window and had been running all night while the rest of the house was 100 degrees, as it's always hot in South Carolina during the summer. In my mind I am thinking, can you please open this bedroom door so that we can all enjoy the air conditioning? But I knew better than to ask that question because it would get me kicked out of the house which may not have been the worst thing. The phone sat on a desk near my grandfather's bed. At that time we used an old school rotary phone. It was plugged into a wall jack, and you had to dial by placing your index finger inside a circular opening on the number you wanted to dial. There were other phones out during this time; some were digital, while some were touch tone but my grandfather liked this one specifically because he could stop you from using it whenever he was not at home. He had placed a lock on the phone. The lock went between the circular openings so you could not dial the phone. "Dang it man," I said! He locked the phone! I ran out of the room in disgust, and my oldest sister Toshia was sitting on the bed. I flopped down beside her in defeat and she said, "what's wrong with you? "I went to use the phone and it was locked. I can't do anything around here; I can't wait to leave one day. I can't use the phone because it's locked, I can't eat because there is no food, I can't sleep because it's hot as hell, I can't think because the house is overrun with rats and roaches, mold growing on the walls". Immune to my complaints, she said, "You have to wait until you go somewhere else to use the phone," she said. He often did things like that and life was not easy in that house. I learned many life lessons living on Edwards St. Most of these lessons started with my grandparents. My grandfather, had a lot of anxiety and stress running a house, filled with people who didn't work, that he had to take care of. He worked at a plant all day and would seldom stop off at the bootlegger's house before coming home, for some liquor. He ran a tight ship at home, and his way of controlling what we did was to monitor the heat, air and food. His intention was good. Daddy-O wanted to keep these things in line so his bills would not be so expensive, as he was the only person in the house who worked. But his extreme measures many times felt like punishment for living. It was getting to the point where I felt helpless. It was beginning to feel like no matter what I did I couldn't enjoy the simplest things in life. With conditions like this at home, doing well in school was something I was not thinking about. I would dream about leaving Edwards St. and never coming back. I thought about suicide at one point. Maybe my family would be in better shape without me at home. One less mouth to feed, one less person to take care of but where would that leave my sisters? I would take care of them from time to time, and they would need me in the future. I am positive there is no way I could take my own life but I certainly thought about it. There were times when I wondered what I was going to be when I grew up. There was plenty of violence and drugs being sold all around me. It's hard to think about the future when the present is filled with so many distractions, and you begin to believe that what you see every day is pretty much going to be your life story, but you have to remember one thing. At any moment we have the power to rewrite that story. At the end of the day, when all is said and done, the only person that is responsible for making sure you succeed is you. This may come as a surprise. Many of us think our parents are responsible for making sure we succeed. The role of your parent or parents is to make sure your basic needs are met. Their goal is to put clothes on your back, food on the table and provide you with a place to live and hopefully you get some love and affection in there as well. Here is the catch, no one ever said the food had to be steak, the house had to be a mansion and that the clothes had to be designer. If someone has provided you with these things, that's great! Do not take them for granted. Please understand that you have everything you need to succeed, if you take advantage of it. The mansion provided by your parents is not yours. The steak you are eating may not always be available to you, the designer clothes that are being provided to you may not always be there so, be thankful if this is your current situation. At some point in your life, you are going to leave those things behind and begin to forge your own way in the world. You will have to create your own path to steak and designer clothes. The question becomes, what are you doing every day to prepare for that moment? Educating yourself and having a plan for your life is something everyone needs to start thinking about, regardless of your financial situation because things can change at the drop of a dime. It does not matter how you start life's journey, what matters is how you finish.

The beginning to my start in the journey of life was not the easiest. Born three months premature weighing 2lbs, I came into this world already battling health issues. After weeks of hospital stay, I went home to live in a small two bedroom house on the Westside of Sumter, South Carolina. In order to create more space in the house to accommodate all the people living there, we put two more beds in the dining room to create a third bedroom. This was a common area between the kitchen and the living room and everyone in the house walked through this area all day and into the night, and there was never any privacy for a young man growing up. The house had no air conditioning in the summer and no heating system during the winter. During the summer we had box window fans to keep cool, but they just blew around hot air and in the winter, we used a wood stove, kerosene heaters or the kitchen oven to stay warm. The house was poorly insulated and I often wondered why we didn't move and get a place of our own, but my mom just could not afford it so we lived with my grandparents for years and eventually moved to a small house on the west side and then finally to Gamecock Apartments, which was income based housing. I often felt like my circumstances were overwhelming but deep inside; I knew I had to find a better way to live. We never had enough food and if you were not around when the food was being cooked, then you just didn't eat. My grandfather kept a master lock on the refrigerator where he kept all the meat and other food items. There were times when I would stare at the refrigerator and wonder "why is this happening to me", but I realized everything happens for a reason. Whatever challenges you may be facing can and will get better if you start focusing on overcoming it. It's hard to believe when you are constantly frustrated and confused about why things keep happening to you, that don't seem to be happening to anyone else? Your life can and will get better if you do two things. The first thing is to believe in yourself and verbalize the fact that something bigger and better is waiting for you somewhere out there in this thing we call life. The second thing is to understand that you are exactly where you are supposed to be. The beginning of your journey does not define who you are. The word beginning is defined as, a point in time at which something starts. Each one of us will start life off on a different path. Some of us will start off in single parent homes, some of us will start off in two parent home with a mom and dad. Some of us will start off in foster care; there are many different ways to start the game of life. The good news is it does not matter whether you start with a disadvantage or an advantage. It does not matter what your situation is, you still have the opportunity to begin shaping your future by doing the second thing. Focus on creating good positive behaviors every day. Moving your life forward to a successful path is possible because it matters not how you start, it's all about how you finish in the end. Every day we are all given a brand new day. Then we get a new week, a new month and a new year if life last and we are lucky enough to see it. The ability to start over is one of the best parts of life. No one is perfect and even though it seems like your parents or teachers want you to be perfect, they really don't. They do, however, want you to be the best person and student you can be and they only have your best interest in mind. I know I am beginning to sound like a parent, but this part will always remain true so read it again and let it soak in. Many people have started out in unfavorable circumstances, many are famous that you may have heard of but there are many role models and people around you every day, that are not famous that you can look up to and aspire to be like. When I think of role models I think of a winter program I once attended as a youth. School was out for Christmas break and I went to a program at the YMCA and there was a youth speaker, who came in to give a motivational speech. I didn't hear a word that he said. He was well dressed and wearing what looked like an expensive watch, well-groomed hair and was well spoken. All I could think about was how this guy grew up. He probably had it all as a child; he was probably spoiled and didn't even have to work too hard, I doubt that he ever missed a meal and he is going to tell me how I can have a better life. Then he began to speak about growing up in a poverty-stricken environment. His story sounded a lot like my own, but yet he was able to lift himself up, change his life and re-write a new ending to his story. I volunteer at a local high school from time to time. This particular time was for an annual College

Day event, and after speaking to a small group of students in the library, I stayed for a while to talk to some kids with questions about going to college. As I was leaving, I noticed one student, sitting alone at a table. I went over to him and asked if he was ok. He looked at me and said, "I have a lot going on, but one day I want to end up in your shoes." He was not in the room when I gave my presentation, but he was commenting about my appearance. I sat down beside him and said, "You are already in my shoes." Let me explain.

## #MinutewithMarlo: Decision

### Your Journey and Successful Influence

1. Do not let your start dictate how you will finish.

   Write 1-2 sentences about your personal start to life. Whether you got off to a good start or a rough start, how do you want your journey to end? Share these thoughts with a mentor, teacher or family member and talk about ways to finish on top!


2. Think about one person that you know personally that you would view as successful. Who is this person? Would you like to be mentored by this person? Ask a parent or close adult to help you facilitate this conversation

# Chapter 3

# Recognize Your Gifts

My 4<sup>th</sup> grade year, I attended Alice Drive Elementary School, I was 9 years old. One of my teachers realized that I was a little smarter than I was letting on to be. I had been passing all of her tests and I was not having any academic problems in her class. One day she pulled me aside and said, "Marlo, I am going to recommend you up for a gifted and talented program". Immediately, the mere words rattled me. There was no way on earth, I was about to be in some smarty arty class, with no friends, no talking, no goofing off, I am sure I would have to do a lot more work than I was currently doing, no way I am thinking to myself. I couldn't come up with a response fast enough. I was confused as to why she would think this is a good idea. The work in her class was easy. I am not sure why but it just made sense. "Mrs. Hooper", I said, "I can't go to another class this late in the year umm maybe, before I could finish" she cut me off "It's for next year don't worry, you will have to take a test to decide whether or not you will be able to transition into the classes". Oh lord! All I could think about was what my friends were going to say when I am in these smarty arty classes! How could I walk the streets of the West Side and who is going to hang out with me? I had to come up with a plan to fix this and before I knew the test date had rolled around. I didn't bother telling anyone at home because I was getting out of this. The morning of the test they called my name over the loudspeaker and I had to report to the cafeteria for testing. Now here I am, this is the opportunity of a lifetime. I have a chance to elevate my learning by testing into a gifted program with focused instruction, smaller class sizes, everything that would make an engaged parents heart skip a beat. However, in my mind, it was the worst thing that could happen. Ridicule, laughing and teasing which would lead to fighting if I had to start wearing pocket protectors and glasses. When the test started, I just sat there. Then I had an idea! Turn the test sideways and start filling in the scantron which is an electronic answer sheet. I finished the test slowly along with everyone else. I did open the booklet, but I never read one question. I had predetermined that talented and gifted was not me and that there was no need to interrupt my class schedule for the next year. When the scores came back, Mrs. Hooper found me. She was very disappointed that I didn't make it into the gifted program. She told me to continue to work hard and that I should never give up. Things will go my way if I just stay focused because I was a sharp kid deep down inside and she knew it. Well, at first I was not bothered one bit by her statements. She doesn't know me; she doesn't know that I don't always eat at night; she doesn't get the fact that I have to share a bed with my mom.  She doesn't know that during the winter my house is so cold in the morning, that I put my clothes on the night before and slept in them, so I didn't have to change clothes in the morning. I came up with a lot of excuses about why I should not have been in those classes because deep down inside, I knew I had missed a great opportunity. I could not see or understand being in that environment because it frightened me and it was something I knew nothing about. None of my friends were testing into programs so it was not even on my radar. I went on with life as I always did. Years later I wondered what would have happened to me had I gotten into that honors program? Don't ever be afraid to share your gifts with the world. If you are talented and can do things that others cannot do, don't be afraid of what people are going to say about you. Embrace your gifts, whether they are physical, academic or artistic. Each one of us has a special talent that only we can share with the world. Higher level coursework is designed to pull your talents out and position you, so that eventually you can make the best of your skills. There will be times when you will have to stand alone and make tough decisions. People may laugh at you; people may make fun of you for doing the right thing. Others may make you think that what you are doing is wrong and not cool. You have to remember what we talked about earlier. At the end of the day, the only person that is going to take full responsibility for your well-being ultimately is you. A crowd is formed when one person occupies a space and others slowly join. Instead of avoiding the things that will benefit you because no one else is doing it, embrace those things and let the crowd form around you. Be the leader that you are destined to be. Many times we as young people hold back our true talent and abilities for fear of what will be said about us. We fear judgment from our peers which could lead to rejection from some social circles. Embracing your hidden abilities is much like hitting a homerun to win the big game. I'm sure you have seen a movie when the main character takes all his energy, and all his focus is on trying to do one thing, hit that baseball as hard as he can then all of sudden whack! The ball goes out into deep left field, over the fence and the whole team runs out onto the field and lifts him up on their shoulders. Did you know that feeling could be achieved by embracing your natural abilities? If you are academically inclined, do not hide it, instead pass every test you take and be proud of your grades, do well in school, do not be ashamed to make an A in your class. If you can sing, join the choir. Do not be ashamed to join the choir because it's not what everyone else is doing. If you can act join the theater club and get involved in as many plays as you can, don't ever be embarrassed to put your natural abilities on display because these gifts once displayed will shape you into the person you are supposed to be. It's okay to admire other people but first, admire yourself. When you have high self-admiration and self-respect, you can begin to shape how people treat you. If you are negative, you will attract negative people and you guys will all be negative together. But if you are positive and upbeat, you will attract others who are positive and upbeat, and those people will support the things about you that are special. Singing, math, sports, photography, and science all those things fall into your special gift category. Everyone has a something they can do well, it takes some longer to understand what their gift is, but as you grow as a person, your gift will become clear. Early on think of your gift as something you are good at doing and something you enjoy. ***#Minutewithmarlo: Decision***

## Do Your Best and Recognize Your Gifts

1. Never be ashamed to do your very best in school. Are you doing your very best in school?

   A. If yes, how do you know?

   B. If not, list one thing you can do to start performing better.

2. We all have special gifts, things that we are good at

   A. What are your special gifts?

   B. How can you start using these talents in order to grow as a person?

# Chapter 4

# The Vision

"Y'all act like money grows on trees around here!" My mom said as she as took a pull from her Newport. She was lying on the couch watching the young and the restless, one of her favorite daytime soap operas. I had become familiar with Victor and the whole cast as if it was my favorite summer show. "What's for lunch?" I said, "I am hungry, we all hungry". My sisters and I had the talk about who was going to go ask mom about getting us fed. No one liked to ask this question because we often knew the answer was going to be one we didn't want to hear. This was often an issue for us especially during the summer when school was out. "Why didn't y'all get up and go to the Bernie Center and get that free lunch like y'all did yesterday?", she. "Man momma," I said, "We woke up late and by the time we got up there it was too late to get on the list to eat free so we missed it." You should have woke me up early! "Boy watch your mouth before I knock you into next week." My mom said, and she meant every word. She was not mean at all but when she spoke she was serious. She laid across an old couch in the living room. It had a flower pattern on it. The armrest and back of the couch was soiled from laying on it with jheri-curl styled hair. My grandfather gets outrageously mad after drinking and coming home to look at those stained chairs that he spent his hard earned money on. The cushions were starting to tear as she repositioned herself to lean forward to address me, her eyes never left that television show as we had this conversation. The sweat was beading up on her eyebrow because the living room felt like it was approaching 100 degrees. She got up and grabbed an old piece of mail. She took the envelope that the mail was in and tore it in half. Sitting on top of the old floor model television next to the cable box, was a pencil. She used these things to draft a small note. She sat down and began to ponder for a few minutes and then she began to write. It didn't take long to complete this assignment. My sisters and I knew all too well what was about to happen. Before she could say it I belted out very sarcastically, "I don't care which one of y'all takes this note, but here you know what to do." She smirked at me and leaned back to finish watching the soap opera. The note was like kryptonite. My sisters and I had often taken these notes to Father Tony over at the Catholic School and that was my destination for the day. I didn't want to draw straws or talk to my sisters about it, I figured that I knew the drill as much as anyone else and as the man of the house it was my duty to take the note. As I walked up the street I pulled the note out so my story could be consistent with the note in case I needed to do any extra begging, just in case the note didn't work. Sometimes, I would rub my stomach and wince in pain, or sometimes I would just sit on the steps of the convent looking as pitiful as I could and wait for the priest or anyone for that matter to arrive and pass them the note. The note said, "Can I please have some spare change until the first of the month, when my check comes in? We don't have any food and I would appreciate it, thanks". I was embarrassed and ashamed to have to be the bearer of the note but it was life and I was hungry. I was extremely lucky on this day because Father Tony was on site. I walked up the steps and the front door was already open as if he knew I was coming. I didn't have to ring the doorbell because he saw me and motioned for me to come in. As I raised my arm to pass him the note, Father Tony shook his head and gently said, "No need for that son, are you okay", he asked, "Yes sir", I said. Good, was his response. He walked over to a huge Folger's coffee can that was glistening with silver coins, all bulging over the top of the rim. He dug in and pulled out a fist fill of quarters, nickels and dimes. I held both of my hands out as if it was Christmas. The coins hit my hands and overflowed onto the ground. I stuffed the coins in my pocket and picked up the ones that hit the floor. I was overjoyed and thankful that I didn't have to do anything more but show up. No long speech, not many words just a pure act of kindness from Father Tony who knew the situation I was in. I have solved the problem for lunch but I was already thinking ahead to dinner. I'll be glad when school is back in session so I can get at least two meals a day. My mother loved us and we loved her just as much. We knew it because she told us regularly. There were times when we had to reach out to other people to ask for help and this was one of those times. At least she sent me with the note and had a solution for the problem on this particular day. Many people helped me from time to time but none more than my grandmother Carrie Prioleau. Carrie was my father's mother. She stands about 5'4, petite in size and soft spoken. She was my grandmother but did many things to earn the title mom as well. She would come visit me on Edwards St. She kept close tabs on me over the years because I was her first born grandchild, a title that she took very serious. I came to know her very well and I spent just as much time at her Frank St. home as I did at my own house. In her care I would learn how to cook, wash cars, cut grass, paint, sweep and mop, wash dishes and clothes and maintain the house. She believed in working hard and saving your money. She often told me this, "If you have five cents in your pocket, and you owe someone five cents, then you don't have any money." She paid her debts and had high moral standards. Many of the skills that I use to govern my life to this very day, I learned from her. Eat, pray, work and behave these were the unwritten rules written on the hallway of the house she built and paid for while working at Exide Battery Company. Carrie is the type of woman who would turn off the heat in her own house in the middle of winter because she knew I didn't have heat in the house I was living in, and she couldn't bear the thought of being warm while I was cold. She stood with me in solidarity for years. She allowed me to stay over at her house anytime I wanted to and most importantly she told me to call her if I ever needed anything. We came up with a code phrase. Most nights I was too ashamed to call and ask her to bring me a meal but we developed a few words that I could use to let her know what I needed. If I was hungry I would simply call and say "my stomach hurts". No less than an hour or so later she was at my house with a hot meal. Most times, it was something fresh off her stove like, baked chicken, macaroni and cheese, pork chops, liver in gravy or my favorite spaghetti in a big Mt. Olive pickle jar. Other times I would make the call then go outside and wait for her to show up. I would get in the car and we would ride to Shoney's, Quincy's or McDonalds. She never asked any questions about why I didn't eat or what was going on she just did what she thought was the best thing to do. My grandmother introduced me to the concept of putting other people first. She knew about the struggles that I had and was prepared to help me in any way she could. She never spoke negatively against my mother, and I was thankful for that because my mother was a good person with a good heart. She was a young, single parent of three trying to survive and make her own way in the world the best way she knew how. As you begin to grow there will be times when you need help and you should not be afraid or ashamed to ask for it. Different people will definitely come into your life to help you along on this journey. It is up to you to recognize when the chips are down and pick up the phone and contact the people who are there for you. It may be your turn to take the note to the church, but if it means survival and it stops you from doing something you should not do in order to make ends meet, it's okay. There were times when I didn't make the call, or take the note but I stole small items from the homes of people I knew, and from local stores just to make it. Those decisions could have landed me in a lot of trouble but each time I seemed to slip away with no major consequences. There were other people around me willing to help, willing to lend me a hand had I only taken them up of the offer. These negative experiences like many of your own happened for a reason. As you grow older you will gain an appreciation for the good times and the bad times. You may be in a situation that forces you to miss out on some of the basic things you need to get by. On many of those nights if I ate or didn't eat I still kept on going. Sometimes, even with the help of my grandmother I had to lie down and go sleep on an empty stomach. During those times I thought about how bad and unfair it was, but I also thought about how one day I would have so much food in my refrigerator that I would feed someone else's kids, which I have done over and over and will continue to do so as long as I am able. I thought about the day when I would not have to ask for money from anyone because I would be able to take care of myself and have all the things I wanted. It was during those times I braced myself and said no matter what, I am going to rise above this situation and make it to a better life one day. Those times served as fuel to a fire I had burning inside of me. I didn't understand it at all at first, I just knew I wanted to be different and I wanted to have a different life. I would visualize a nice home, a nice car and think about being able to take care of myself and not have to ask anyone for anything. Thinking about the vision and the end result is what gave me hope. I wasn't sure how I was going to get there, I just knew that one day something big was going to happen to elevate me out of this situation and that one thing ended up being, a college degree.

*#MinutewithMarlo: Decision*

**Key Influencers and Self Visualization**

1. Who are the people in your life other than your parents that you can turn to when you need help?

2. Visualize your life as an adult? What does it look like? Where do you live? What do you do for a living?

# Chapter 5

# Negativity

"Marlo, you ain't never gonna be nothing!"
Grandma Liz had a way of reminding me that of the
seven people she had living with her on Edwards
Street, in our small two bedroom house that, I
wasn't her favorite and she wasn't shy about letting it
be known. My mom had three kids and we all have
different fathers. A lot of anger was directed at three
innocent children because of this. My grandparents
often reminded my sisters and I that there was really
no reason we should be living in their house. "You
think because you talk smart you know it all and
because you know some white people you special?,
Well you ain't. When you around those white people

you look like a fly in a bottle of milk" my Grandma Liz said. "Get out of my way". She would say things like this at any given time whenever she felt like it. At thirteen years old it was hard to swallow and difficult to understand. She pushed past me, exhaled the Newport in the direction I was standing before she went into the kitchen. The white smoke was so thick that it almost choked me. All I could do was make a tight fist and grit my teeth before heading out into the streets for the rest of the day. "One day I'll show you," I said, underneath my breath as she walked away, then I took my hand and smacked my butt, the smack was a little louder than I thought it would be, she then began to slow down as if she had heard exactly what I said loud and clear. "Did you just tell me to kiss your ass"? She took one last look at me through those black rimmed glasses, curly wig and cigarette hanging off the tip of her lip. She drew back her hand and brought it down across my face.

POW! My head whipped to the right but I didn't stumble I just stood there with tears in my eyes. But I could not give her the satisfaction of crying or being in pain. She strolled on into the kitchen as if her job was done. As I headed out the door I heard these words in my head, words she used on me often, too black, too dumb, too short, too ugly, and too poor to amount to anything good in life. Sometimes, people will direct their failures and shortcomings onto you and they'll say things to belittle you, but they are really disappointed with their own life, and don't know how to handle their own frustration for their shortcomings so they take it out on people that are closest to them. I can't blame her, she is forced to deal with her own children who have fallen short by not graduating from high school and now they have children who have needs that must be met and no one has any money or structure to move the house in a positive direction. Everyone was frustrated and the negative comments were always directed towards my sisters and me. The more you hear something the more you start to believe that it's true. As I got closer and closer to graduating from high school I would debate over and over whether I was good enough to make something out of myself. I kept hearing her words to me over and over. I started to wonder if they were true or false. In this particular moment, my thoughts had won, they had gotten the best of me and my self-esteem was beginning to fall to its lowest point. I needed to get out of this environment fast. I left the house and jumped on my bicycle. I rode all the way to my Grandmother Carrie's house non-stop. By the time I got there I had completely calmed down. I didn't want her to be worried about what was wrong with me. Her house smelled like spices all year long because she constantly baked cakes, pies and was an excellent cook of anything.

She had a huge yard that I would mow with the riding lawn mower or push mower whichever was working at the time. She gave me a big hug and smile as she greeted me at the front door. This was real love and it felt amazing. Everything about this environment was right. There was food, it was comfortable, clean and relaxing. When I was here I had no worries. There was no one selling crack outside, there was no fighting in the streets, no loud music just birds chirping, wind whistling and gospel music playing from the radio. In these moments, I realized that it wasn't me that something was wrong with. I was the same person who was just told I was never going to be anything; I was the same person who watched his neighbor bash her husband's head in with a 2X4 piece of wood in the front yard. I was the same person who snuck in my other neighbor's house to steal some food and whatever else I find. I was the same person who was ducking down on the floor at the masonic temple during a shoot-out. I was the same person that the police surrounded and drew guns on, slammed on the ground and searched in the sporting goods store because there was a report that I was dressed like a gang banger and was packing a gun while walking through the mall. That day I realized it was my environment that was causing me so much pain. Being in that house, in that neighborhood limited my options and forced me to deal with certain elements that I didn't have to deal with at my Grandma Carrie's house. I started realizing that I was not a bad person, but I was not in a perfect situation. If I could change my environment from time to time eventually, I could have this feeling of relaxation all the time. When times were tough, I would look for refuge in different environments that were positive and uplifting. Instead of talking back and fighting with people who were negative toward me, I began to ignore the comments, and I started thinking about ways to prove them wrong. This became the internal driver that would help guide me towards a better future. I wanted to prove every person wrong that had ever doubted me, talked down to me, viewed me as too black, too short, not smart enough, not dressed good enough, not rich enough, that I could be enough. As young individuals we spend a lot of time trying to be "enough" for someone else. The only person we need to be "enough" for is the person in the mirror. It's so difficult with peer pressure and social media but we have to first respect and be proud of ourselves before anyone else attaches a label or false stamp of who we are on us, we have to be confident in our own abilities and who we are. Now let's be real for a second. I had heard this before as a young man, "You need to know who you are" and all types of other clichés' but I never could figure out how it related to me personally. Well, I would think to myself, I don't really know who I am, don't I have time to figure that out as I get older? The answer is Yes!, you do have time to figure that out. However, if you lean on simple things now such as knowing right from wrong and not being afraid to do what's right, regardless of who is watching you, no matter what your friends or family might say, then you begin to move into understanding how to be the best person YOU can be and how to make the best decisions that are good for YOU. You can live in the worst neighborhood ever, but if you choose to ignore the elements and decide to choose positive actions instead of negative actions, eventually you can change your situation. Those are the first steps. All wisdom is not instantly imparted upon you when you get to a certain age and it doesn't fall on you when you become an adult either. It's a gradual learning but you can walk in wisdom right now by simply by choosing right from wrong and positive vs negative.

### *#Minutewithmarlo:Decision*

## Environment and Negative People

1. When times get tough, do you have a positive environment that you can go to?

   A. If so, where is it?

   B. If not, work with an adult that you trust or close family member to identify a place

2. Do you sometimes interact with negative people and situations?

   A. If so, how do you rise above the negativity?

   Even if it comes from one of your own family members?

# Chapter 6

# Insecure

So Marlo, "What are going to do after you finish high school?" she said. Oh lord, here we go again. As I slumped down into the brown leather couch, I could feel the sweat forming under my arms, my stomach was in a complete knot and my heart was racing. I hated this question with a passion. This was not the first time I had been asked this question in the past few months of my senior year. I didn't understand why this was never brought up before, and it probably was but now that I am a senior it seems to be the only question adults want to ask me. Why are you so concerned with what I do after high school? I might not even make it out of Sumter, SC, was my thinking. "You need to start thinking about the future, it's already your senior year" said Leila as she peered out from under her glasses with a very caring and concerned face. Her voice was gentle and the message was heartfelt. But I didn't care. My response: "I ain't going to college"! I do know that for a fact. I don't really have a plan for after high school. All I really want to do is live to see 18. If I graduate from high school, then I will worry about what my next move will be. I'll probably get a job at the local chicken plant on highway 15. I know plenty of people who make a decent living by working there. Now that answer sounded good…to me. But it was not my true answer. Leila began to do what a good step-parent should do at that point; she gave me a great speech about what I should do and things to consider. She only wanted the best for me, but as usual, I zoned out. All I could think about was getting off that couch and getting down to the corner store to hang out with my boys. All this talk about life after graduation could wait, I mean I might not even graduate because I am not that smart right, or at least that's what I told myself. I left the house that day with sweaty armpits, a wrinkled brow and one thought, "Man, I am not even college material." I honestly didn't believe in my heart that I was capable of achieving any level of major success. I didn't think it was for me because I had not seen or met a lot of people who had attended or graduated from college. The thought of school really scared me and now I am starting to hear more and more about it. I really had not prepared for school, so that made it even more difficult to envision myself there. I had no plan at all. Only what other people thought I should do. I had not internalized my own plan yet, but I was beginning to think about it day. My insecurities were strong and I wasn't sure how I was going to overcome them. I didn't really want to work at the chicken plant but I didn't have any real answers. What if I don't do well, what if I can't afford it, what if people don't like me? This thinking further led me to believe that college was a pie in the sky thing and probably was not for me. I was not quite ready to say yes.

## *#Minutewithmarlo: Decision*

### Current Plans and Insecurities

1. Make a statement below about what your plans are after high school graduation:

2. Do you feel like you are not a college material?

   A. Do you have other insecurities that make you question whether school is right for you?

   B. If so explain reflect on the text and discuss with an adult or someone you trust.

# Chapter 7

# The Plan

"I ain't going to college yo," "I am good!" As I slammed down my ace of spade, then gathered up my book of cards and neatly placed them on the side of the desk in Mrs. Betchman's class. She allowed us to play cards for a few minutes while we packed up and waited for the bell that would send us off to lunch. "I ain't going either man," said my friend Carlos, "that's for them smarty arty wanna be white boys." "I feel you man; I ain't going either I'll probably go into the army or Marine Corp" said my other good friend, Glenn as he peeked over the six cards that he had remaining in his hand. Before we could finish the game, we heard a loud ding…ding…ding sound. It was the bell ringing that signified lunch was ready. As I walked away from that 4th block English class in 1995 headed to lunch my senior year, some of the kids in that very same class were starting to get acceptance letters and were talking about heading off to college in the fall. I could only think of one thing. I ain't going to college, to hell with that. We ate lunch, laughed and joked around like we normally did. I spent more time talking about what I was not going to do after graduation versus what I actually was going to do. High School graduation for me had been a mere dream. There were times that I thought I would not graduate from high school but instead catch a stray bullet or get shot, beaten by the police or go to jail. With graduation right around the corner, I had no idea what was in store for my life. This is when my friends were experimenting with drugs and adults I knew were already hooked mostly on crack cocaine.

The street life was appealing but I knew I could do better than selling drugs. Fortunately, my life changed during one of those fourth-period card games in March of 1995.

A few weeks passed and I am back in fourth block English again playing cards. My eyes were deeply focused on the hand I was about to bid and I was suddenly interrupted by this deep stern voice coming from the front of the room. As I look up and over, I see a man, small in stature, with a huge pair of glasses and very low haircut. His eyebrows were thick and his voice was heavy, as I looked up his eyes connected with mine and he said "hey you! come here and let me talk to you for a minute." I am thinking I don't know this guy, what does he want with me? So I don't move. I look around the room as if to gesture that he is talking to someone else and not me. He then says, "YOU, COME HERE BOY!" By now my friends are looking at me like dang dude, what in the world did you do this time? I start walking over to him slowly, as he leans further inside the door frame. "What is your name and who is your mother?" he says in a very stern voice. I am thinking this dude is going to call my momma what the hell is this about?! "I am Marlo and my momma name Rosetta", I said as discreetly as I could. I didn't want my friends to hear how this conversation was going to end. He then said something that surprised me; He asked "what are you going to do when you graduate?" I am standing there in the doorway of 4th block English being asked the very question that everyone is dying to know the answer to. Fortunately, I had the answer to that question ready to go so I blurt out. "I ain't going to college." He then says, "I understand, it's not for everyone". I am thinking finally someone who understands and is on my side! This guy is alright with me. He then says, "would you like to go on a trip this Thursday?" At this point, I am confused. I am thinking to myself, I just told you I don't have a plan, and now you want to take me on a trip? So I asked, "is there going to be food on this trip?" He nodded his head and those thick eyebrows moved up and down. I took that as a yes. I motioned with my head and he understood that I was interested. By the way, he said, "My name is Anthony Graham; you can call me Mr. Graham." "Yes sir," I stated. He then said, "Do you have a shirt and tie?" If not, borrow one from someone and instead of reporting to homeroom on Thursday come straight to my office at 8am". I agreed and off he went with his glasses sitting on top of his head. I went on to lunch that day, never thinking about or questioning where we were going or exactly what we were going to do. It didn't matter, I knew that food would be involved and I would certainly be there.

Looking back on that day, I realized how important it is for a young person to have a plan. A plan requires proper preparation; I didn't have that either. But at that point, I started to realize my days were numbered and if I was really going make anything out of myself, I needed to start by analyzing what I was going to do upon graduation. Planning is a key part of life for students and adults. Not just having a plan but writing that plan down on paper with clear goals and objectives will help you navigate life's path. Life is about natural progression. Most people will journey from elementary school, to middle school, to high school and then beyond. You already know certain things are inevitable therefore; one should create a plan for after high school. A plan is your intent to do something with a purpose. There are no mistakes in life, everything that happened to me happened for a reason. I had no plan for after graduation, and I had done minimal work in high school to actually prepare for college. I didn't know how to study, my grade point average was low, and my course work was weak. Later, all these nuances would come back and plague me in the worst way. Create a plan for yourself as early as you can. The plan should change as often as your mind changes and should serve as a blueprint for your life with a goal of knowing exactly what you want to do and where you want to be two to three months after you graduate high school. Below is a short sample plan that can serve as a foundation for college planning specifically:

| Freshman Year | Sophomore Year | Junior Year | Senior Year |
|---|---|---|---|
| Parent Conference With Guidance Counselor | Join School Clubs and Organizations | Narrow School List | Apply Early Start During Summer To Top Selections |
| Maintain a Minimum GPA of 3.0<br><br>College Tours | Participate in Career Days<br><br>College Tours | College Tours | Focus on School Cost Specifics<br><br>Tour Final Selections |
| Develop Good Study Habits!<br><br>Search and Apply for Scholarships | Start Having Conversations Around a College Major<br><br>Search and Apply for Scholarships | Start applying for College Scholarships<br><br>Search and Apply for Scholarships | Learn About Financial Aid-FAFSA<br><br>Search and Apply for Scholarships<br><br>Complete Financial Aid |
| Select Course Work College Preparation Track consider<br><br>2 year or 4 year schools | Create Top 10 School List | Collect 2 References One Guidance Counselor 1 Teacher | Make Final Selection<br><br>Start Planning for Life On Campus or Off |
| Practice Test PSAT/ACT | Take: PSAT/ACT | Take: SAT/ACT | Take: ACT or SAT |

If the military is of interest to you, then start practicing on the ASVAB as early as your sophomore year of high school. Take it early for practice and take it over again to achieve the score you want.

## #*Minutewithmarlo: Decision*

**The Plan**

1. Use the chart to give you some idea of what you can start focusing on to make college a reality.

2. Don't limit yourself to what you see here. Use your phone, laptop or mobile device to help you road map important pieces of the college entry puzzle.

# Chapter 8

## Positive Influences

On Thursday, March 16th 1995, I arrived at the school bus parking lot. My grandmother drove me over and as she drove she asked me a few pertinent questions. She said, "where are you going?" I said in normal teenage language, "I don't know." And it was true. I never bothered to ask where we were going or what exactly we were doing. It didn't really matter to me. It was something to do other than skipping school, only to walk up and down Edwards Street or get into trouble. At that point I was a senior in high school, with no real plan; no money saved up headed on a trip with no idea where it was going or who was going to be there. I had it all figured out. NOT! Up until this point, I had no real thought about what my next steps would be. Grandma told me "you are about to be a man, it's time for you to start thinking like one." At that moment, as I stared out the window I started thinking about the men I knew and had spent the most time with. My dad was the first person I thought of. Unlike most of my friends I knew exactly who my father was and I even knew where he lived. My dad lived in California. I would visit my dad during the summer when school was out. He was hard on me when I saw him because he knew his time with me was limited. He always encouraged me to do the right thing and always stressed that school was important. He would say over and over that I needed to go to college and he was very serious. He wanted the best for me and he did the best he could for me, when I was with him. My times in California were awesome. It was like living two lives. He took me to Disney World,

SeaWorld, the movies, and the circus. Things I would never do back in South Carolina. It was hard to enjoy it all sometimes because at the end of the day I knew reality would set in and I would be headed back to Sumter to once again face the challenges of meeting my basic needs. I enjoyed myself and tried not to think about home. I knew my sisters were facing the same issues and because I was not there, I would pray that things didn't get any worse for them. My dad loved me and we had great times together. He taught me about having respect for myself and he echoed hard work just like his mom. Visiting my dad was like going to a movie. It was exciting and fun for a few months and then it was over. But I am glad I went because the movie would play over and over in my mind during some of the tough times, back at home. He had not gone to college yet, but swore to finish before I graduated from high school so I would have no excuse. He did just that graduating with his degree from Pepperdine University before I finished high school in 1995. My Dad grew up different from me. His mom, my grandmother worked hard to make sure he had the things he needed. He didn't live in a rat and roach infested home like I did. His house didn't have mold growing on the walls like mine did back in Sumter. My dad did the best that he could and I appreciated that. It was more than many of my friends could ever say. I valued his opinion but it was always hard to understand his perspective on things because I felt like his life was so different from mine. I often wondered if he did realize the things I had to deal with at home. Did he realize as he slept comfortable in his California apartment that I would go home to a house full of people to share a bed with my mother. Years later I realized that my Dad's role was to expose me to the finer side of life. He was my barometer and he showed me that I could have a better life and that more options were available to me, regardless of what I saw every day. Unlike most of the people around me, I had above average experiences and my dad was solely responsible for that. As I came back into focus, I could feel the car starting to slow down as we approached the intersection at McCray's Mills Rd, I turned away from the window as I heard my grandmother's soft voice say, "Baby we almost there." Ok, I replied. As I sat up in the dark burgundy Buick century with my grandmother behind the wheel and I began to stare off once again. Another man popped into my mind Mr. Anthony Hayes or Uncle P as I would call him. He was married to Mary Ann who was like another mom to me, and I was good friends with Shawn and Toray, their two sons. In the hood, I considered them to be rich. They had two cars, a house and were married. This was one of the few men I knew in the neighborhood personally that did not have a blended family. Uncle P worked took care of his family and he even spent time regularly with me. I went to his house almost every day. The boys had their own room, two beds, cable television and plenty of video games and toys. Going over to Uncle P's house was a treat. I would often eat there and spend the night. He always had a word of wisdom for me and I always listened because he was one of the first men I knew and was around on a regular basis that took his family responsibility seriously. Nothing was more important than his wife and his kids. He kept his boys in the latest clothes and sneakers and most importantly he kept them together under one roof. I would often wish I was a third son but it didn't matter that I wasn't because he treated me just like a son. He is one of the reasons that I vowed never to have any children until marriage. I saw the way his house ran with order and no drama and that's what I wanted for myself one day. Suddenly, my whole body jerked forward and then back into place, "oweee" I shouted out loud. "if you were paying attention you would have noticed that large speed bump we were about to go over", said grandma. "What in the world are you thinking about?" She asked. "Nothing", I said. We had arrived at the school and were moving through the parking lot. "Do I need to get out and talk to someone about where you are going?" "No, ma'am", I said. It's a school trip. She had a blank stare on her face but she agreed, be safe, there were no cell phones back then so I told her I would call from the school once we returned. I jumped out the car still thinking about being a man and what that meant to me. Then I saw my good friend that I had known since 6th grade, JD. "What up, Jay?" I said with excitement as now I have a familiar face for this trip to who knows where we are going. "Nothing much man, just chilling," he says. I liked JD for a few different reasons. His parents were divorced and his mom was an educator so he was on the straight and narrow path for the most part. He was also a student athlete and well-liked by all. We came from two different backgrounds but we both had one thing in common, we both liked to party and hang out! "Where the hell are we going?" said JD. "Man, you think I know! I just came because I heard there was going be some food and I wasn't really doing anything else so that's my excuse". He nodded as to agree. He then said, "Well, my momma called the school, because when I told her I wasn't sure where we were going, and that I just needed to be at the school, she thought I was up to something," he said. We both burst out into huge bellowing laughs. JD's mom is no joke. She stays close to whatever it is that he has or thinks he has going on. "Boy your momma closer to you, than a diaper on a baby's butt! If you have the info on this trip, tell me where we going," I said. "Man Lo, since you got jokes, you will have to wait and see", he said. I sat down on the curve and we waited for about fifteen minutes and then a yellow school bus slowly pulled up and the door opened. By this time more boys has joined the group and about fifteen of us in total started to gather at the steps of the bus. Standing on the bottom step of the bus was the man that had sought each one of us out individually and made sure that we were available on this Thursday morning, Mr. Anthony Graham. He was a small thin man with thick eyebrows, perfect teeth and a stone look on his face. I had only interacted with him once before, which was the day that he invited me on this trip. As we stood around the bus door anxious, loud, and behaving exactly how a pack of wild teenage boys should on a school-less Thursday morning. Finally, he scanned the crowd of boys all dressed in different colored shirts and ties and then in a deep stern voice he said,

"Listen up!" We stopped dead in our tracks as if the police had just yelled, Freeze! It was starting to warm up and some of us had already taken our shirts out of our pants and loosed up our neckties: "Straighten yourselves up right now. From this minute going forward you are a representation of me and I am not taking anyone with me whose pants are not up around their waist, with a belt on looking sloppy. This is not a game we have important business today and I will not let you embarrass me or yourselves. Do I make myself clear?" We all started checking ourselves, tucking in our shirts, making sure our pants were not sagging, adjusting our ties because we knew he was not playing. It didn't matter where we were going if we wanted to make the trip we better straighten up right now or get left behind. We boarded the bus one by one. As I took my first step, Mr. Graham was there to shake my hand, "you look nice son," he said, "thanks" I replied. He made sure everyone was sitting down in their seat and we had instructions to talk softly and not move around too much. A few of us were brave enough to play a few hands of speed in between the seats until we grew bored of that. Once again, I found myself drifting off out the window as we cruised down I-95. I began to reflect on the statement my grandmother had made. I could hear her saying it again, "you are about to be a man, it's time you start thinking like one!" Once again, I started thinking about the men who I spent the most time with and thought about Mr. Salvador Macias or Uncle Sal as I used to call him. I met him one Halloween when I was about seven years old out trick or treating in a neighborhood far away from where I lived. I saw this nice house on the corner of Church Street and I knew some good candy was probably in there. My friends and I went to the door and two small boys came running to the door along with a short, stout man. He had long curly hair and brown eyes and thick beard and mustache and next to him was a very short brown haired woman with blue eyes and a warm smile. I knew the candy would be awesome in this all white neighborhood of Sumter, but I did not know this couple was going to help change my life forever. "Trick or Treat" I said and then I realized as I put my hand out for the candy, these boys went to my school. It was Mike and Tony Macias. I played with them at school and they were my friends. I had no idea this is where they lived. "Hey guys!" I said with excitement. They said hello and we spent some time talking. Mr. Macias said, "Marlo, you can come visit us here anytime you want." I starred inside the big house with the dogs and I looked up at his sincere face, I knew instantly that I needed to return to that house very soon, and I did. I am not sure what it was, something about these total strangers drew me in completely. Years later I realized I gravitated towards married couples because that structure and life was what I wished I had. I received peace knowing people had solid family units and it gave me hope that one day I could do the same. I spent so much time with Uncle Sal, his wife Lucinda or "Mom" as I would call her eventually. It was like I had inherited another family complete with a mom and dad who went above and beyond for me on many occasions including helping me complete my seventh grade science project, feeding me numerous meals, driving me to and from school and even allowing me to stay in their home for extended amounts of time when the worries of my world on Edwards Street were just too much to bear. Here is a couple that didn't look like me, but was an integral part of my whole life. I saw in him another man that took care of his family, was educated and was there for me regularly when I needed someone to talk to and lean on. In that moment, I started realizing that the men I needed to look up where not on television, they were not on the radio but they have been around me my whole life during different times and in different situations starting with my father. JD and I were sitting in the same seat and after a while he nudged me with his elbow and said, "hey man are you alright?" Yeah, I said, "I just have a lot on my mind. We're about to graduate in a few months, what the hell am I going to do? My mom dropped out of high school in 10th grade, went back to school and got a GED some years later and I was very proud of her so she has something to work with. My dad is out in LA working, has his own place and is married so he has taken care of himself for the most part. My grandmother is retired; she is doing her thing and is taken care of. My aunt Carolyn went to school but she was smart and had good grades and is already into her career, so she is taken care of. But what about me, what in the world am I going to do?" JD just stared at me as if I was crazy. He looked at me like, dang man, why do you have to make this so difficult. Then he says, "man I was having a great day until you brought all that up." He threw his head against the back seat of the bus and closed his eyes. He was college bound because both his parents went to college. The worries and ills that I had he didn't have. I want my children one day to rest easy like JD, and know that their paths are predetermined to a certain extent. I didn't want them to experience the frustration and fear of not knowing how all of this was going to work out. This trip began to make me think about something that I have not really thought about in the past, having a family one day and being educated enough to take care of them. There is an African proverb that says "It takes a village to raise a child". My village was strong. People will come into your life for many different reasons. They fill roles that are missing;

they may serve as unofficial mentors and way makers. They serve as examples of things you should and should not do, but it is up to you to evaluate these people and choose certain pieces of what they represent and implement those pieces to your own life. Allow the positive things to fuel your next steps and help you grow as a person. Too many times in our community we look for role models in the wrong people. We idolize people who will never be in a position to know our names let alone serve as an example of someone you should want to be like. Your village is very important, there were many people I could have gravitated towards but I choose positive, family oriented people who were doing something that I viewed as special. Some people you will choose, others will choose you.

## *#Minutewithmarlo: Decision*

### Positive Influences, Mentors and Family

1. Who has been a positive influence in your life and why?

2. What positive traits can you take away from these people that can help you have a better life one day?

3. One day you may have a family of your own.

   A. What type of educational experience do you want for your children?

# Chapter 9

# College Tour

As my eyes opened from the cat nap I took, I saw a sign that said, Orangeburg. We started to exit the highway and the others started to wake as we started hitting traffic lights on highway 301. We weaved our way through this small rural town, and we all woke up just in time to see this huge sign that said, SOUTH CAROLINA STATE UNIVERSITY. I looked at JD; he looked back at me puzzled. I blurted out "Mr. Graham has brought us to a college! What in the world for." This is last place I was thinking about going. All I heard as we took the right turn into the campus was moaning and groaning from the boys. But all that soon stopped because as we peered out the left side of the bus a group of girls were having a photo shoot of some sort on the steps of the Martin Luther King Jr. Auditorium. Our attention was immediately captured and we knew we were about to see something special. "Yo, you see this!" says JD, "yeah man I see it and I would like to meet it, you feel me!" I said with a smile. We laughed and started looking around as the bus drove into the campus. The school itself was amazing. It was like a scene out of a movie. The lawn was manicured, the buildings were regal, some nostalgic and others modern. This was the first college campus I had ever been to. I heard about people going to STATE, but I really didn't make the correlation that these people were talking about South Carolina State University. Students were everywhere. Kids were laying out in the grass reading, others were gathered under trees laughing and others were engaged in a conversation that you knew was important and intellectual by the nature of their faces and their posture. I was completely in awe of these students and I also realized something about this school that made it different but inviting. I was at a Black College or a HBCU as they called it. We would learn more about this later. At South Carolina State University everyone I saw looked like me. Their skin was as dark as mine, some of them were as short as me, some were skinny like me, some had coarse hair like me, they wore clothes similar to the ones I wore to school and they really didn't look too different from my friends and I. It was shocking! I always imagined college students with sweaters tied around their necks, the most expensive clothes, nice clean haircuts, glasses, loafers, khaki pants, button up polo style shirts, and jewelry. Some kids were outfitted that way. I actually saw a young kid driving an older BMW, which was mind blowing because I am pretty sure he didn't sell drugs to get it. College kids were normal! We pulled up to the Washington Dining Hall. It was very clear this was the place to be. Students were sprawled out all over this particular area. Some were sitting on the brick wall that ran in front of the cafeteria. Students were steadily moving in and out of the cafeteria with purpose. The atmosphere was amazing. Mr. Graham stood up and made the announcement, "Listen Up, we are at South Carolina State University, this is college life and we are about to experience it in full. We will walk amongst the students, eat in the cafeteria, see the dormitory as well as the rest of the campus, I don't want any problems or you will be sent back to the bus, is everyone clear on that?". "Yes, sir", we couldn't wait to get off the bus and see what this place was all about. We exited the bus directly in front of the cafeteria. As soon as we walked off the bus, we were greeted by Jabar. He was the student body president. He was wearing a pair of jeans and a SC State t-shirt. A group of students gathered around us and started asking us questions such as where we were from, what grade we were in and what school did we attend. For one of the first times in my life, I felt like a star. People were genuinely interested in me and my point of view. Total strangers who did not know anything about me wanted the best for me. They only wanted to see me do well and if they could answer any questions I had they were fully prepared to do so. I felt as if I had found another home right there at South Carolina State University. We toured the entire campus; Jabar asked us what we knew about HBCUs, he was met with silence so he began to explain. HBCU stands for Historically Black College or University. We later learn about this in more detail. They talked to us about state supported schools like University of South Carolina which is a predominately white school, Morris College and

Claflin University which are private HBCUs and are funded differently from the state supported schools. We even talked about private predominantly white schools such as Furman and Anderson University. Jabar took the time to educate us on colleges in general which he didn't have to do, but he wanted to make sure we had an understanding of higher education, which most of us did not have. I was thrilled, even more of a reason to be interested in this school. We ate in the cafeteria and ended at the office of admissions.

## *#Minutewithmarlo: Decision*

## College Visits and Types of Colleges

1. Have you ever visited a college campus?

    A. If yes, where did you go and what was your experience like?

    B. If you answer no, work with an adult to visit a  school nearby so you can begin to see what college is all about!

2. Familiarize yourself with the different types of schools.

    A.Public Colleges & Universities, Private Colleges & Universities, HBCUs, Public and Private. Research one example of each:

# Chapter 10

# Realization

Getting in was now my question. Deep down inside I knew I wanted to attend SCSU, but my defense mechanism was to refuse it and not let anyone know that I am really interested because I know I didn't prepare properly for college. As we sat on the steps outside the admissions office, I stared up at the deep blue sky. JD was sitting next to me and he asked, "Lo, are you going to go here?" I looked at him and said, "naw man this ain't really my style". Instead of jumping for joy and screaming as loud as the SC State 101 marching band, I remained calm. "It probably cost too much anyway." I was thinking of other things I could say so JD would lay off and not ask me anymore questions. "Man, you see these girls," he said? Those two over there, man that could be us man, come on". I played it cool because I didn't want to be too excited in case it didn't pan out, "Them chicks don't want us man, look at them guys they kicking it with". One had on a jacket that was red and white and had funny letters on it. "What kind of jacket is that", I said to JD? He knew a lot about college and college life. His village had prepared him well. "Man those are the Kappa's. It's a fraternity ya know?" "No, not really" I said, he began to talk about Omegas and Kappa's and I began to fade into those blue clouds. The peacefulness of the campus, birds chirping, sunshine smiling down on us felt so good. There were no broken bottles on the ground, no old needles left in the grass from the junkies that had been there previously, no broken windows or graffiti written across deserted houses, no patches of dirt where the grass didn't grow, no drug dealers standing around waiting for the next car to drive up so they could fight over who was going to make the sale, no cars sitting on cinder blocks, no box fans in the windows, no smell of marijuana in the air and no one fighting in the streets.. just kids going to class trying to pass. JD eventually started laughing with another boy who was on the trip and they struck up another conversation. The more and more I watched those young, educated kids walk past me the more and more I wanted to be like them. But I wasn't sure if the university was ready to have me. I started thinking about all the things I should have done, and now it's too late. I thought back to how I choose my classes at Sumter High School. I remembered some kids in my class saying that they were going to take college prep classes so they could be ready for college when the time was right. If only I had done the same thing. If only someone would have told me that taking *Mathematics for the Workplace,* was only going to teach me about counting money and cashiering maybe I would have listened. If only someone would have told me not to take *English: Communications For The Workplace,* I could have skipped the humiliation of tearing my homework out of a workbook to be turned in like a 3rd grader. The teacher for the class Mrs. Hampton often let me work with other kids in the class who were having problems with the material. English was one of my best subjects. I sat in the front the class, which gave me my first opportunity to instruct other people. I made straight A's in this class and it was partly because of my unofficial role. Secretly, I knew she needed me to explain things and work with other people in the class. That meant more to me than the class itself. Finally, someone who I felt was of public importance a teacher, thought I was important. I knew I could have done better work in a higher level class but when I enrolled; my main goal was to graduate with four English credits. Looking back on it, the class was not about satisfying an English credit, it was about me getting some emotional satisfaction and learning how to feel like a winner with an important leadership role in the classroom. I don't know if Mrs. Hampton did it on purpose or not, but she did it. The next year I took the highest level of English I could take and I did just fine. Once again, I had taken the low road and now I was starting to regret it. What if South Carolina State University would not accept me? I spent four years of high school dodging the hard classes; I had a history dumbing down, not working as hard as I knew I could. Now that I was closer to making this huge decision the self-doubt started to settle in. I remember it like yesterday. We completed our applications by hand while sitting on the steps of Wilkinson Hall and we turned them in before we left. Little did I know my future had been pre-determined and this mighty institution would change my life forever. As we departed the school, I was not sure if I would ever return, but what I did figure out in those few hours was that college was, in fact, the perfect place for me and I wanted to come back. I wanted it more than anything I have ever wanted before and I was now on a new mission to get into this magical place of educational harmony. This was a place where I could grow and actually escape the ills of the community that I had grown up in during the 80's and mid 90's. College was a different world where people wanted to be in class, achieve more and be successful. A place where a young person could get the support needed in order to grow into an adult and live a life that he or she never dreamed of. I was so excited about this that I couldn't believe it. College was becoming a possibility, and that's all I could ask for as I began to take the necessary steps to making it a reality. It's important to give life and positive energy to your possibilities which are things in your life that have a chance of becoming real, accept those ideas, believe that it can actually happen, and tell people about it because the more you talk about it and visualize yourself doing it, the closer you will be to making the possibility a reality.

## #Minutewithmarlo: Decision

## Pushing Yourself and Exploring Possibilities

1. Are you pushing yourself to take challenging classes?

2. Do you know what the proper classes are that will best prepare you for college?

3. Have you ever made a good grade or been excited about something that happened to you at school but you did not share it with anyone? What was it?

4. What possibilities are you thinking about that could one day become your reality?

5. What steps are you taking to make the possible a reality?

# Chapter 11

# Starting to Believe

My grandma Carrie was waiting for me at the school when we returned. "So where did you go?" She said with a smile on her face as if she knew something good was about to happen. I was actually excited, "I went to South Carolina State University" I blurted out. Right after I said it, I sat back in my seat almost embarrassed about what I had said. I felt a little ashamed that I was now excited about college as I had not been before. I had changed my mind and grew up in a few hours. Everything that I thought about college was wrong. Everything I thought about the type of people that went to college was wrong. My entire view and thought process about higher education were all wrong. "What!" She said "that is the same thing as "State College" right? She said with a puzzled look on her face. Yes, I told her, the name had changed a few years ago from State College to State University and I had learned that on the visit. "So you want to go there?" She said. "I don't know yet, it's alright", I said as I stared out the window. Even after seeing the school and having a total revelation about the school I was still hesitant to share how I really felt. As a young man trying to find his way, it can be very hard to express how you feel to adults, even the ones that are close to you. She knew something had changed in me on that trip but she didn't force the issue. Instead, she started talking about something that all teenagers want to hear. "You know", she said in that soft voice of hers, "going to college is a big responsibility you are going to need a car to get back and forth if that's something you are thinking seriously about doing". I slowly turned my head towards her in complete surprise with a confused look on my face. Somehow going to college equated to getting a car. That's basically all I heard. She made a few more statements but the rest went in one ear and out of the other. A car would change my life. Even if college didn't work out I would still have the car. This was a total game changer. Even though I had already decided to attend college I still did not have a plan in place as to how to get there or have any idea how I would survive once I got there. I was not ready to share my new point of view just yet. I needed to think some more about how this was going to work out. As school continued over the next few weeks I started hearing phrases like SAT and paying for college. After visiting a SCSU I knew I needed to take the SAT, but had no clue about how to register for it or where it would be held. I needed someone to help me figure this next step out. I found Mr. Graham in the guidance office. He told me to go see my counselor if I wanted to take the SAT on the next available date and If I had any issues to find him and he would take care of it. I went to see my guidance counselor for maybe the second or third time in all of my four years in high school. I went to the office and the secretary told me who my counselor was and she scheduled me an appointment. I went during my fourth period English. I did remember Mrs. Wilson counseling me before. She was a very young looking counselor. She stood about 5'2 and had long dark brown hair. She was very serious "Mr. Marlo, how are you?" She said. "Fine" I answered. "I need to take the SAT, so what steps do I need to take?" "Well, let's take a look at your file" she said. Aww man, I am thinking in my head once she looks at "my file" she is going to stop me from taking the test. "Let's see" she says in very monotone voice, she took a long pause.... "you have not met the

Math requirement for college prep, but you did meet the math requirement for graduation, same for English, Science and Social Studies. Do you realize the SAT is going to be pretty difficult being that you have never taken Algebra 1, Algebra II or Geometry, Or four College Prep English courses, nor Chemistry?" I interrupted her because I wasn't in the mood to be questioned about the obvious. I already knew I had an uphill battle and I didn't need a reminder. "Just tell me how to sign up for the next test. I heard I could take it for free because I eat free lunch, is that right? Also, can I get a waiver, because I don't have any cash right now?" I said. Her eyebrows went up, she realized that I was serious and I could tell she was about to give me all the information I needed. "That is correct" stated, Mrs. Wilson. She gave me the date I would be taking the test and suggested I take a SAT prep course or at least get a SAT study guide from the library; I did neither. She signed me up to take the test on Saturday, May 3rd, 1995. I did not ask any additional questions, our meeting was short, sweet and to the point. I was a little surprised that she didn't give me a long speech about not doing my best, but I sensed that she knew what position I was in and didn't want to make me feel any worse. She told me to come back if I had any other questions. My last few months of high school I tried to do the best I could, turning in all my assignments on time, actually studying for test and passing them. Of course, at this point, it's too late to have any substantial impact to my GPA. I felt like time was running out for me. Real life was approaching and I still had no real plan of action. I had not taken the SAT, graduation was right around the corner and I had all my eggs in one basket. My Aunt Carolyn was another crucial part of the village. She was like my big sister. She was twelve years older than me but she was around Grandma's house a lot and we spent a lot of time together. Whenever she came into town she would be sure to pick me up or let me know she was going to be at my grandmother's house so I could be there. She always asked how I was doing in school, how was I doing at home and if I needed anything. She never hesitated to take me to the store and get me whatever I needed so as I started talking college this was no different. She jumped right in as I began telling her where I was in the process. She had gone to Winthrop University and suggested I look into it since my mind was now open to attending school. A few weeks passed and she took me to Winthrop University for a visit. As we walked around the campus, I admired it. It was spacious and green, with lots of students all scampering around the campus for the summer session. The dorms were massive and the cafeteria was immaculate, but there was something missing. I couldn't tell exactly what was missing because this school had everything you could possibly want and more. I didn't rule Winthrop out but I was pretty sure the school I wanted to attend was going to choose me and I wasn't going to have to choose it. Sometimes you just have to believe in yourself, I knew on paper I didn't have the typical college profile and the odds were against me. I knew the SAT would be hard and I would love to say, that I spent the next few weeks studying feverishly, studying every second I could for it, but I didn't. Instead, I rested on the fact that everything I needed was already inside of me, and somehow it was going to work out. I believed that I was going to succeed and make the right score on the SAT and that I would be offered admission to college. I began to reflect back to my guidance counselor visit. Everything she told me was true. She said nothing that I was totally unaware of. She was simply trying to set an expectation for me so I wouldn't take failing the test so bad. But she failed to realize was I was betting on myself, I was going to do well and I was going to make it no matter what. I had to accept the facts that I had not prepared myself and it was my own fault. I took responsibility and all I could do was move on and focus on the SAT. Life is going to present you with many situations that may not be in your favor initially. There may not be anything you can do except move forward and focus on the big picture. If you let words and circumstances break you down, your possibilities will never become realities. I could have been defeated in that office but because I had made up in mind that I was going to continue to fight this fight regardless of my history, I was not discouraged. Let your frustration be your fuel, let your mistakes be your mile-markers and let your disappointments be a lesson on what not to do again. If I made it to college I was going to be sure to challenge myself and not make the same mistakes again. I was also determined to not let where I started dictate where I ended, it was time to write a new a chapter in this book and I was ready.

## *#Minutewithmarlo: Decision*

### *Starting To Believe*

1. Whether you were in a situation where the odds are against you or not, maybe you didn't prepare as you should have for the test, recital, final exam, project or SAT, once you determine that you are going forward, you have to believe in your heart that you are going to win.

Think of a time where you did not prepare but came out victoriously in the end and write about it below. Use this as fuel if you are not the most prepared to take that next step after high school to college.

2. Think about a time you were very determined to change an outcome or a situation you were in after being told you could not do it.

A. What was the situation and what was the outcome?

# Chapter 12

# Wrong Place Wrong Time

Graduation is now upon me. I only had two weeks left before I walked across the stage and accomplished a major feat in my life. Two Saturdays before graduation I decided to go out to a party. I called my partner James that morning to make sure he was still going out with me. I had spent the night with my grandmother so I had access to a phone and I was pretty sure I was going to be able to drive her car, as long as I did my chores at her house she had no problem letting me borrow the car. That morning she surprised me yet again. Today we are going to go look for you a small car, she said very calmly. I jumped up from the breakfast table filled with hot grits and eggs that she always made me and said, YES!! I was so excited because I knew there would be no looking only. We would walk away with a car today and I was driving my own car to that party tonight. I had it all figured out. I finished my breakfast while grandma pulled in a load of clothes off the line that already been outside for a few hours because she had gotten up early, washed clothes and cooked breakfast for me. My only task for the day was to mow the lawn and wash her car. I mowed the lawn and washed the car in record time that day. What normally took me a few hours seemed like only a few minutes on this day because I was about to make history by becoming a car owner. My mother, Grandmother Liz, not even my older sister had a car. Up until this point, we walked and rode bicycles everywhere unless my grandmother Carrie Prioleau drove me. My Grandfather had a car but no one was allowed to ride in it and he would not take you anywhere, so there was no need to ask him. We headed out to Broad St. to see what we could find. On our way to the car lot, my grandmother Carrie asked me a few questions to make sure I wasn't sliding back on our agreement. "Did you hear back from State College yet?" she said as she looked over at me while I was driving. "No, ma'am, not yet. Hopefully, my SAT score come back soon and I'll hear something", I said. Hoping that was good enough to continue the drive and not have her mind change all of a sudden. I didn't look over at her because I didn't want to see her facial expression. "That's good, I am sure God will work it out, if life lasts" she said, which is her normal response to everything, such as waking up the next day even though she was in perfect health. I had no expectation of what type of car I was going to look at. I was going to take and be happy with whatever we looked at; I could care less as long as it worked and was mine. We drove past a few car lots and pulled into a Mazda Dealership. There was a used section and new section. We parked the car jumped out and headed to the used section to see what we could find. Needless to say after a few test drives and some mean negotiations by my Grandmother we left with a 1993 Mazda Protégé, my first car. There were no words to describe what had taken place that day. I never imagined owning a car before graduating from high school now I have to make it to college at least for a year or two just to show my gratitude to Grandmother Carrie for making such a huge investment into my future and my life as she had always done for me. That night I was ready to party in style. I couldn't wait to pick up all my friends and break every rule that my grandmother has given me as we sat in the office at the dealership completing the paperwork.

It's Saturday night and I am ready to party. I called James and he answered the phone, his tone was low and he didn't sound good at all. "What's wrong with you man?" I asked him. "Man, I got in trouble and I am on punishment. I can't go anywhere tonight. Matter of fact here come my momma now about to tell me to get off the phone, so I'll catch you later." Click, he hung up. I didn't get a chance to ask him any questions or anything. So instead of calling around to see who else was available, I'll just head out solo. I'll see some people there I know, so it's not a big deal. Sometimes it's better to travel alone in your own car so if something happens I can take off without having to look for anyone. I got ready to go and my grandmother gave her full blessing to hang out for a few hours that night because all my chores were done. I jumped in the car and put on one of my favorite rap song's AZ's Sugar Hill. I had it on full blast as I rode through Sumter headed to the

Masonic Temple. I pulled up and lots of cars were in the parking lot just as I imagined. I was under aged but they never really check ID's, I should get in with no hesitation. I walked inside and I didn't see as many familiar faces as I thought I would. I saw a few people I recognized from school but none of my immediate crew was there. I walked around for a few minutes checking out the party and people were dancing and having a great time. The Dj was playing all the radio hits and I was bobbing my head and walking around looking for a dance partner. I ended up near the bar area not too far from the dance floor, looking around to see if any familiar faces were in the club, there always was. I ran into my friend Tia; she had dropped out school because she had a baby. We talked for a while and had a good laugh. She was facing me and my back was turned to the dance floor. Suddenly her eyes began to widen with surprise. I turned around and standing right in front of me was a guy I never saw before. I immediately balled up my fist thinking it's about to go down. He leaned in real close and said, "Remember that night you had me face down in the dirt with that gun pulled on me" HUH! No one was really paying us any attention, by this time Tia had walked away. I said "naw man, I don't know you like that", as I put my arm up to push past him he pulled up his shirt and it was the black handle of what I knew was a gun. As he took a step even closer he pulled the gun out and had it down by the side of his leg, the barrel of the gun was pointing straight down, I froze, I started thinking how could I get to my car, I had come too far to end up like this. I was college bound; I had just received my own car, I was doing as good as I could in school only to get shot at a party! As the strobe light shined on my face the gunman took a good look at me with the gun out in his hand but down by his side and not pointed at me just yet. He then says, damn man, I thought you were someone else. He tucks the gun in his waist and walks off. I had cheated death that night because he could have shot from anywhere in the club thinking I was someone else. The music was so loud that I just needed time to think. I walked to the other side of the club and just leaned up against the wall to catch my breath. After about a fifteen minutes; I calmly left the club and headed home. Sometimes in life you are going find yourself in a compromising position. Every action has a reaction. At 17-years-old did I really belong in a nightclub? This could have been the end of the road for me, my life lost and the world would have moved on as if I never existed. There were times when my step mom used to tell me, "Just because you can do something, doesn't always mean you should." Every year in the news there are reports of teens that die or get severely hurt due to no fault of their own. Over the years, I found myself in a lot of places I should never have been, which allowed me to see and experience things at a young age that I really didn't need to see or be involved in. I was in the wrong place at the wrong time, luckily it end well for me. Looking back on that senior year I was in a lot of places I should never have been. I did a lot of things that I should not have done. Sometimes bad things happen to good people because of the choices we make. You don't necessarily have to be doing something wrong for something wrong to happen to you. That's why it's important to keep your nose clean and stay away from places that you have no business being in. Had the outcome of that night changed for any reason, if he decided that I was the person he thought he had an altercation with and started shooting from across the club, this book would have not been written and I would not have made it to college. That night I learned that there were certain places I was supposed to be at age 17 and some places I was not. Anything can happen when you are in the wrong place.

### *#Minutewithmarlo: Decision*

**Don't get caught in the wrong place at the wrong time.**

1.  Have you ever heard the phrase, wrong place at the wrong time?  How can you avoid being in the wrong place at the wrong time?

2.  What if all your friends are going and counting on you to be there, but you know the environment is not safe, how do you handle that?

# Chapter 13

# Accepted

I graduated from Sumter, High School in June 1995 and I was extremely thankful. Many of my friends that started the journey with me did not make it across the stage that year or any other year. I was now done with school and all I had to do was get into college, preferably at South Carolina State. At this point, I fully realize that any bad decision I make at this point going forward could impact my future. What was I going to do now? I was able to get hired at the local grocery store. Many of my friends thought that was a good enough job and that if I stayed there long enough I could "move up" and I would have no more worries. I could live the life I had always dreamed of living right here in Sumter, SC working as a bagger for Piggly Wiggly for the rest of my life. Many of my friends who did graduate with me were not working over the summer and had no plan of going to college or doing anything that I knew of. One day in late June after I worked 7am-3pm pushing out groceries in the hot South Carolina heat, I decided that I needed a definitive answer from State. There was no way I was going to bag groceries as a career. All I could think about were the kids I saw, hanging out in the cafeteria, driving around the campus and the love I felt when I was on campus with Mr. Graham. I had to have that feeling once again. Once I got home, I jumped on the phone and called the school. "Admissions, how can I help you?" said the woman on the other end of the phone. My Name is Marlo Prioleau, and I am waiting to find out whether I am accepted or not? She said, If you have done your application on time and submitted all your scores and transcripts you will receive a letter in two weeks lettering you know your admittance status. "Ma'am, please, I can't wait two weeks, I have to get into this school, I don't have any other plans this has to work out for me, is there anything you can do to help me?" Two weeks she said, I hung up the phone. I couldn't believe I wanted this to happen so bad. I went from having no plans, to South Carolina State being my only plan. Every day for the next two weeks I checked the mailbox and I had my grandmother checking on the days I was not there. Maybe I had set myself up for disappointment. I started thinking that maybe I still wasn't college material and that all the reasons I didn't want to go to college were true and maybe I tried to fool myself into believing that I really had a chance at a higher education and a better life. Those were the worst two weeks of my life. But I needed those two weeks to strengthen my belief that what I was praying for and waiting on was about to be the best thing that ever happened to me. On July 18th 1995, I went to the mailbox and finally found a letter from South Carolina State University addressed to Marlo Prioleau. I tore the letter open right there while standing at the mailbox. As I read it, the tears started running down my face. I had made it and I knew my life was going to change.

*"Congratulations and Welcome to the Bulldog Family! You have been granted admission into South Carolina State University."*

I was accepted into South Carolina State University and school was going to start in exactly four weeks. August 18th was freshman move in day and I couldn't believe I was headed to Orangeburg, SC. I went inside and started thinking about all the different things I had been through. From living with my grandparents among rats, and roaches, sharing a bed to our low income duplex in Gamecock where gunshots rang out at night. I thought about all the nights with no food, my mom leaving my sister Toshia and I with my grandparents who made us wash our own clothes in the sink with a bar of soap and find our own meals, to be being hit in the face and told I would never amount to anything, to being on the verge of a clean slate. I was about to leave it all behind. No more sharing clothes with my sister, borrowing money from people just to get by and pay bills. No stealing food from my neighbor's house, or wondering where my life was going to end up. There was something about this next step that I could feel in my soul and everything about it felt right. I used to always say "I ain't going to college." I would say it all the time but the truth of the matter was my father had whispered college into my ear as a child, and for years I wondered if what he said was true. "It's the only way son, I promise you", he said. I saw my father a few times a year mainly during the summer but he always left me with that message. The morning of August 18th, my aunt Carolyn and my Grandmother Carrie drove me to South Carolina State University. I wore a XL white t-shirt with Tommy Hilfiger across the chest, jean shorts and a pair of white reebok classics. It was a hot Carolina day and everywhere you looked people were scrambling trying to figure out the next move, where to go, what to do and how to do it. I saw all my black people, intelligent, smart, studious, bright eyed, ready to go. They were asking questions and getting answers. Administrators were helping people register for classes and get financial aid taken care of. It was a whole new world and I realized one thing. After my aunt, Carolyn and grandma helped make up my bed they said goodbye. Grandma put a few dollars in my hand as always and asked me if I was ready. Well, I said, "they let me in so that must mean they want me to be here." Once they left, I sat on the bed and looked around. My roommate had not arrived yet, so I went outside and stood on the sidewalk of Bethea Hall. I looked around at all the other students like myself and I came to one conclusion. No one here knows me. My past has been erased. They don't know about how I grew up; they don't know how much money I have, they don't know about the house I grew up in, they don't know about the sleepless nights. They don't know about the algebra I, chemistry and geometry that I never took, the foreign language I failed, the mistakes I made in high school, all these things were in the past. There were no preconceived notions about me. I was free. This allowed me to be who I really was. There was a person hiding inside of me all these years, a smart, ambitious young man with big goals and dreams. There was a huge challenge in front of me and I was ready to accept it.

Have you done things in the past that you are not so proud of? Your past is your past for a reason. It does not define you; it only creates and shapes the person who you have grown to be. Many times in life we find ourselves going through different situations, some good and some bad. Always remember this...10% of life is what happens to you, 90% is how you react to it. This simply means it matters not what happens to you, because as long as you walk the earth you are going to find yourself in challenging situations from time to time, what matters is how you respond to it. Ultimately, it's you who determines the final outcome of your situation. No one has the last say over where your life ends up except you. No one can respond to a situation pertaining to you except you. In a young person's life, there are defining moments; these are times in which you make a decision that is going to impact a major part of the journey you are on. For me, the first defining moment was going on that college tour. That literally changed my life. The second defining moment for me was standing on that sidewalk after my family left and deciding that no matter what happened to me from now henceforth, I was going to do four things: Be myself, get involved, have fun and graduate. Little did I know that my self-declaration would all be fulfilled beyond measure for the little boy from Sumter, SC.

# Chapter 14

# What Did I Actually Learn In College? 6 Life Lessons

As you matriculate through whatever program you choose you will gain book knowledge. There were many lessons that I learned that did not come directly from the text books. They were life lessons, some hard lessons but I still appreciate each one to this day.

## Lesson One: Expect To Succeed

When I skipped my 8am English class I didn't realize anyone would care. It's college right, the land of creating your own rules and forging your own path. I had no idea that my teacher was going to call me to ask, why I wasn't in class, I had no idea she would send word via my next door neighbor that I better be there tomorrow! I had no idea that she would do everything short of sending a smoke signal to make sure I received the message that missing class- your freshman English class was not an option, for it was the gateway to understanding how to manage your time, be responsible, adhere to a schedule and be accountable to yourself. Do what you are supposed to do even when you think no one is watching because at SC STATE the expectation was not to fail, but succeed beyond measure. The expectation was to attend as many classes as possible, the expectation was to do your best at all times. I had to learn to set expectations for myself. I did that by graduating with my degree in Marketing. I accomplished that by not missing many more of my classes not just English and doing my best at all times. I did not graduate from college overnight. I was able to obtain my degree one day at a time, one class at a time by setting high expectations for myself. In life often we sell ourselves short by not expecting much. We do enough to get by, enough to stay off the radar, enough to not get into too much trouble but we have to take a stance and become deeply grounded in the fact that we can be great. Our ancestors were great and we come from a long line of successful people. You may not see them every day, you may not hear about them in school in all of your classes but you were not put on this earth to be average. You were not put on earth to wear your pants down below the waist. You are not just here to be teen mothers or fathers. You are here to make a positive impact on society! We all have a purpose in life and the power to fulfill it. You must expect more out of yourself and hold the people around you accountable by expecting them to be better. We have to go back to a time where taking care of each other as brothers and sisters was expected, as well as having high standards for how you live your life.

### #Minutewithmarlo: Decision

## Expectations

1. What expectations do you have for yourself?

2. What goals do you plan to achieve regarding plans for after high school?

## Lesson Two: Follow Up

As I sat in the auditorium on August 18<sup>th</sup> 1995 as an incoming Freshman Cynthia Zieglar, Sherry Mack-Michael, Rudine Howell and Joseph Thomas appeared on stage inside the Martin Luther King Jr. Auditorium. They talked about internships and the importance of the career prospecting process. As they talked I began to see myself in a suit and tie handling business affairs and jet-setting all over the country. Everything they said about preparing your resume and having the best interview skills all made perfect sense. I viewed these people as the gatekeepers to my success even though they were perfect strangers. I wanted every ounce of knowledge that they had about these so-called internships that I was unfamiliar with. At the end of their speech, Mrs. Zeigler said, Don't wait until your senior year to come see us. Come now! The very next day I was at the South Carolina State University

Career Development Center located at Nix Hall. The staff members I mentioned above were waiting to receive me with open arms. I received three paid internships while working on my undergraduate degree. Upon graduation, I had three offer letters or full time employment from those companies. Sometimes you need to listen, absorb the information and follow up on it. Whether you are sitting in an auditorium, standing in line at a game or having a conversation with someone at an event you are attending, listen to what the person is saying and If good advice is given act on it. Too many times we interact with people, get great advice but fail to act on that advice. Don't let the conversation fall on deaf ears. Take action and you will be surprised at the outcome.

## *#MinutewithMarlo: Decision*

1.  I want you to think back and recall a time when someone gave you some good advice? Did you follow up on it, or not? What was the outcome?

## Lesson Three: Don't Give Up

Sophomore year I arrived on campus more excited than ever to be heading into my second year of college. Campus was crowded and students were everywhere trying to register for classes, obtain housing assignments and move in. I went over to the housing office located in a little white house right across from Bethea Hall. I suffered through the line and finally reached Mrs. Connie Shivers director of housing. She scrolled through the records, looked directly into my eyes and said, your room deposit was not paid! I am so sorry, baby. I walked outside and almost collapsed in the grass. How could I not have a room! I went to the student center and called my dad. He confessed that money was tight and that he had indeed missed the deadline to pay for my on-campus housing. When I walked out of the phone booth, I saw my friend Tony G! He was in the same boat as I was. We drove around all day looking at apartments and talking to people who could help us. We ended up at Colter Room and Board. This was a huge house within walking distance of campus. The house had close to 12 large rooms inside of it plus an office, two bathrooms, and one kitchen. I wasn't too fond of the idea of living off campus. How was I going to eat? How was I going to pay rent and bills? I didn't have a job and I relied heavily on financial aid to pay for school. I began to think maybe all of this was this is sign. Maybe I should pack up and go home. I did one year of college and had a ball. I made some new friends, learned about some new ideas and topics that I had never thought about before and maybe this was all I was supposed to do here. Maybe my purpose had been served. I started to give up. I sat on the steps of Colter Room and board and started thinking about going home. What would I do if I go back to Sumter, SC? I could hear the stories and whispers about Marlo. He went to State but he came back home like the rest of those so-called college boys. He came home just like we thought he would. Then I realized this was just a minor setback. I decided on those steps that I wasn't going to drop out of school but instead, I was going to find a place to stay at all cost and I was going to do whatever it took to stay in school. I got up off those steps and went inside Colter Room and Board and secured a room with no money down! Mr. Colter said he would work with me and that I shouldn't worry. I spent six months in that room and it was the best six months of my life, not because I had a place to stay but because I didn't give up! My declaration was almost compromised, but I stayed the course and kept my focus on graduating. I can't graduate if I drop out, right!

## #Minutewithmarlo: Decision

## Never Give Up

1. Name a time you almost gave up but you pushed through it instead? What happened and what was the outcome?

## Lesson Four: Don't Just Achieve Excel!

1996 was my sophomore year of college. I was already walking in my purpose of educating myself at all cost and exercising my personal declarations when I started looking for my very first summer internship. I had visited the career development center at South Carolina State many times and I often talk about it because it was instrumental regarding a few different parts of my college career. I started thinking to myself, if this is where all the employers come to look for students for jobs and internships why not spend as much time here as possible. Mr. Thomas, the center supervisor at the time, would let me make copies and run errands around campus. Eventually, I started picking up the phone when no one was in the office and I had an epiphany. Maybe I could get paid to work here instead of working for free. I spoke to Ms. Howell about it and she told me what steps to take, and I did exactly that. Within a week I was hired, and I started working at the center a few hours every day. My first task was to help organize the upcoming career fair. I worked hard on it with the rest of the team; it was a great fair. Eventually, I received an assignment that was too good to be true. In the days following the career fair, some employers were going to set up on-campus interviews for summer internships. I was asked to meet with each employer at the end of the day to debrief with them regarding the interviews they had throughout the day and find out what our students did right and what they did wrong. When I was first assigned this task my immediate thought was "Yes" I'll have access to the employers and I can really get ahead of everyone and know what internships will be available and I can apply for them. I created an exit form, so I could have consistent questions that I would ask each employer to record my data and I was all set. The first day I met with William Lorrick human resource director for JC Penny, out of Chicago, Illinois. He interviewed eight students from South Carolina State and finished early in the afternoon. I went into the interview room and began to question Mr. Lorrick about what he liked and what he didn't like. I asked him questions such as what could this one student have done better? I asked about how the students were dressed, were they professional, did they answer the questions properly? How was their demeanor, and body language? I shook his hand, asked him if he needed anything else from me and I left. That evening as I was re-typing the data up to submit to the center director it hit me...The reason I was there was not only to make connections with the employers but to learn the real do's and don'ts surrounding the interview process. As I read the notes it was as if I was taking a class on interviewing, professional development, salary negotiation, professional dress and some other soft skills. I had learned about these things before in some of my classes but here I am hearing it straight from the horse's mouth. I had the answers in my hand to construct the perfect interview from dress all the way down to how to ask for the salary I wanted. Once again by just being myself, I was now ready to land the internship of my choice. Over the next few days, I interviewed human resource managers and directors from SCE&G, Pfizer and Coca Cola to name a few. Soon after other students started asking me how they should dress for an interview, what should they do and what should they say? I started holding private sessions on interviewing, and I began to really understand what Dr. Stacey Settle had imparted into me during my time in school. He was my mentor from the school of business who believed in me just as much as I believed in myself. He taught me to be well rounded and how to carry myself as a professional. It's great to achieve academically but in order to really excel, you have to take advantage of every opportunity that comes your way. I could have met with those human resource executives, turned in my paperwork and went on about my business but I took it a step further, maximized the relationships I made, capitalized on the information I gathered, used it to help other people and ultimately used it upon graduation to gain employment. Always challenge yourself to do more. Don't be complacent with any situation. Hard work will be out the smartest person any day of week. Going above and beyond will always lead to personal satisfaction in knowing that you did all you could to learn, benefit and grow from any given situation. If your teacher asks you to write a one-page paper, write two pages. If your mom ask you to take out the trash, gather all the trash from every trash can in the whole house, take them out and replace each one with fresh bags, if you are practicing for a sport and you normally shoot 10 free throws, shoot 20. Work on developing an attitude of excelling versus simply achieving. Anyone can achieve but to truly excel you have to diagnose the situation you're in and take full advantage of it. If you practice doing more with small tasks and assignments as you grow and face more complex situations and tasks, your mind will be in a mode of excelling versus achieving and you will go above and beyond. Don't be satisfied with the bare minimum.

### *#Minutewithmarlo: Decision*

### Achieve vs. Excel

1. In your own words, why do you think it's important to achieve vs. excel?

2. Give one example of what you can do TODAY to start training yourself to not only achieve but excel?

## Lesson Five: Be Curious

My junior year I was taking a stats test upstairs in Belcher Hall and this exam was harder than concrete. I felt like I knew the information but I got lost in the formulas once the exam started and there was no coming back from it. I decided to throw in the towel. Once you turn in your exam you were free to go and I walked out of the class feeling totally defeated. Once I got downstairs I realized that I left my stats book under the desk. The book was expensive. I ran back into the building and jumped on the elevator to go back to the classroom that I had tested in. When I got on the elevator, there was a well-dressed man also going up. I was curious as to who he was. He had a professional dark blue suit, black wing tip shoes, white shirt, blue and gray tie.

He was very well manicured, and every hair on his head was in place. I immediately thought to myself this man looks very important. I started to fix myself up. Tucking in my shirt, pulling my pants up a little and I turned to him and said "good afternoon," He looked at me with a huge smile and said "good afternoon young man," how are you? Yes! I was thinking, exactly the response I was looking for. "I am fine thank you; my name is Prioleau, Marlo Prioleau." "Good to meet you, Marlo, my name is Switzon Wigfall." "Nice to meet you, Mr. Wigfall." By that time the doors had opened and he was getting off so I got off as well, even though it was not my floor yet. Can I help you find something, or do you know where you are headed? I am fine, he said. "I was looking for Mr. Thomas but I have been on this campus before." "Okay great," I said very enthusiastically, what are you doing on campus if you don't mind me asking? Mr. Wigfall said, "no I don't mind answering you at all, actually I am the Director of the Black Executive Exchange Program and I am looking for students to complete an internship this summer." Now at this point; he has my full attention, my heart was racing and I was trying to be clever but not come off as too arrogant. I have already done two summer internships so I know I have positioned myself well for this exact moment. "Funny you should mention that", I said, because I was just starting to look for a summer internship! "Oh really", he said. Well, what kind of experience do you have, he said in a very stern voice? I learned how to answer these types of questions before and it was like taking candy from a baby. I talked briefly about the experience of my past two internships and he nodded and smiled. He then said", are you attending the banquet tonight?" I said "Yes, sir". He said "good, we can talk more when I see you there!" and he trotted off. Now as I walked back to the elevator I began to think to myself what type of banquet is this, where is it and how can I get a ticket or an invite! I had no idea what banquet he was talking about but I knew I had to get there. I ran all over the school of business asking my professors about this banquet that was taking place and none of them had any idea. On my way out the door, I saw Mr. Freeman, the janitor. Freeman! I blurted out, what time is the banquet tonight? He said, man, it's starting in about an hour across campus in the garnet and blue room. Freeman always did the setup and breakdown for most school of business events so I had a feeling that he knew, and I was right! I went speed home, cut my hair, ironed my best white shirt and put on my best blue suit and black shoes with the belt to match. I wanted to look exactly like Mr. Wigfall because if he saw himself in me, I knew I had a chance to get that internship. I came back on campus dressed with my business bag, resume and a business card that I had created. As I approached the door of the banquet hall I don't see any students, as a matter of fact, I only see one of my professors. I could see people were checking in with tickets. I came too far to turn back now I had to get inside. As the woman in front of me checked her name on the list at the door, I slipped past her and caught Mr. Wigfall's eyes, he waved his hands in motion for me to come on in and that's exactly what I did. I sat at his table and did the best networking I could. Everything I learned about building relationships and representing myself had paid off in those few hours at that table. I applied for the job officially and a few weeks later I received a letter stating that out of 2500 applicants I had been selected for the Black Executive Exchange Program and I would be representing South Carolina State University! I packed my car, changed the oil, picked up my dad and we drove to Dallas, Texas for one of the best experiences of my entire collegiate career. On the morning of my first day on the job Mr. Wigfall found me. We bonded over the next several months and he took me under his wing along with Greg Cody, Alvin McCrainey and Hazel Weathers. These people were instrumental in teaching me the fundamentals of business and how to conduct myself as a young man navigating corporate America. Earlier, I stated that it takes a village to raise a child, once again the village had taken to the little boy from Sumter, SC and this group began teaching me the unwritten rules about listening and observing, speaking at the right time, professional dress at events of a different nature, handling confidential information and so many other things. Sometimes, you have to go where you are not supposed to go in order to be who you are supposed to be. When that internship ended, I had to write an essay about my experiences while there. I let my aunt

Marilyn read it. Marilyn had always been a great support system for me and always offered a word of encouragement when she was near. She read my paper and had tears in her eyes. I knew that moment I had to continue to do great things and that motivated me to have one of the best semesters at school I had ever had. This time I exercised my best personal declaration, Be Yourself.

## #Minutewithmarlo:Decision

### Be Curious

1. Are you willing to work towards being successful no matter what?  Give an example of how you plan to be curious going forward:

## Lesson Six: Be Thankful

Senior Year nothing could be finer. I couldn't be in a better place. I have positioned myself well, learned so many things and met so many people. I have grown as a man and learned things about myself that I didn't know. I learned that I could be successful, I could be savvy, I could speak well, I could pass tests, I could navigate the business world, I could complete difficult tasks, I could think critically, I could be funny  all the things that I had been told over the years growing up that I couldn't do I did and did well. Graduation was right around the corner in just a few months. My resume solidified me as a young professional and I had no worries about getting a job after graduation. One cold day in February and I had one more lesson to learn about moving forward with life. I answered my phone on the first ring as I sat up in my bed because it was my brother, one of my best friends since freshman year

Tiant Nettles. He said "I am on my way to the Burg man so get up and let's hang out". "Cool," I said. I jumped up and took a shower and made us some breakfast. He arrived from Columbia and we caught up in the living room of my two bedroom apartment. We laughed and talked like we normally do. We came up with a game plan for this beautiful Saturday which consisted of shopping, eating and hanging out with some girlfriends of ours in Columbia. We hung out all day and decided around 5pm to make the drive to Columbia in two separate cars. He led the way in his red mustang as I followed in my vehicle. We weaved in and out of traffic and arrived in the capitol city in no time. He drove to his apartment in Horrell Hill. Tiant was very eager to show me his apartment. He had graduated with honors from South Carolina State and this was my first time traveling to his new apartment as he had only been living there for close to a month. He was a school teacher at a local elementary school and had the best attitude and the sweetest spirit a man could have. I pulled up beside him in the parking space and immediately nodded my head in agreeance. This is nice man! I said, before walking inside. He put the key in the front door and we went inside. It was a very manly apartment. He showed me the downstairs area, kitchen and the living room. I sat on the couch to test it out, bouncing up and down a few times while we laughed about all the fun he would have entertaining friends and family in that living room. We started up the stairs to see the rest of the apartment. We went into his bedroom and I was in awe, my friend and brother had graduated and made it. He had a great job of shaping young minds just like his parents who were educators. He had a place of his own and a bright future. I sat on the bed and said "man I am proud of you dude!" "Thanks" he said and we just laughed because we understood each other. I stood up and headed over to his closet to check out some new jackets that he had bought and all of a sudden I heard a loud thump! As I turned around, I noticed that Tiant had fallen down to the floor. He was a tall, medium sized man and I thought maybe he tripped and decided to stay down for a while to laugh. "Get up man you always tripping on stuff," I said. But I noticed he was not getting up and he was not laughing. I immediately dropped down to my knees and looked at his face, he was non-responsive. My first thought was to do CPR because he was not breathing. I started the process, breathing into his mouth and pumping his chest. I looked around for a phone and realized his apartment was so new that he had not yet installed a phone line. I ran out of the apartment and over to the neighbors to called 911. I ran back into the apartment and continued CPR until the paramedics arrived. I began to drift off at that moment as they worked on my best friend, my brother, the guy who taught me how to change a tire, how to check the oil in my car and where to get an oil change in Orangeburg. The guy I spent every day with for the past four years, riding up and down the SC highways and byways; stopping at thunderbird restaurant to have the best chicken on the east coast was slipping away right before my eyes. All the late nights and early mornings, laughter encouragement to do better, was about to end. Without a moment's notice we would no longer ride together or walk the campus together only in spirit. Tiant Nettles was 23 years young and he went home to be with the lord on that night. This happened on a Saturday. On the following Monday, I had a job interview. I was not going to go to the interview. Everything was happening so fast I didn't even have time to think, but I knew Tiant would have wanted me to keep going as if nothing ever happened. As hard as it was I went to that job interview and I even spoke briefly about what had taken place and I asked the interviewer to excuse me if I seemed at any point not engaged because I very much wanted the position but I had suffered a major trauma. Again, it's not about what happens to you it's about how you handle it that matters. A few weeks later, I was offered the position with SUPERVALU in Minneapolis, Minnesota and I accepted it. In life, the hard times will come. It may feel like life is over but those are the times you have to persevere and stay the course. Keep going and always continue to move forward no matter how hard it is. I often imagine where my life would have ended up had I not taken that job offer, had I not mustered up the strength to move on in spite of what had taken place. What if I had listened to the voices that were telling me to give up, drop out of school, go home. Instead, I remembered that I had made a pledge to myself to graduate, therefore quitting was not an option, no matter the circumstance. I was severely depressed and very sad. This is not what my best friend would have wanted for me. Life is extremely precious. We have to be thankful for each day we are able to open our eyes and have breathe in our body. I share this story in particular because tomorrow is not promised to any of us. Make sure that you are living each day to the fullest with the intention of one day seeing your master plan come true. This situation allowed me to go to a place that I never knew existed; a place of focus, strength, power and peace to face anything. Tiant gave me that and I am forever grateful.

## #Minutewithmarlo: Decision

### Reflection of Life

1. Think back to a tough time that you had to persevere through? A. How did you handle it? B. What gave you the strength to keep going?

2. Be appreciative for the life you have, Are you focused on being successful, making the best decisions that will position you for life after high school? If not what will you do today to become more focused than you have ever been?

# Closing

Going to college proved to be the best thing that ever happened to me. I never thought something that I once revered with everything in my being would end up being the very thing that helped mold and shape me as a person. I learned that it's better to prepare yourself for opportunities and have none than not to prepare yourself and have opportunities presented to you, but you can't take advantage of it because you have not prepared for it. Educating yourself and having a plan for your life after high school is the single most important thing you should be thinking about. School is going to progress year to year from one grade to the next elementary school to middle school, and middle to high school all in preparation for one big moment. For those of us fortunate enough to graduate from college; this is actually the beginning of your life, not the end. This is where the story unfolds and the fork in the road becomes even more defined as you stand in the middle trying to decide to go left, right, or straight ahead. Either way, you are creating a path for yourself and the more prepared you are, the easier the transition into adulthood will be. College for me was more than just a place of learning. It was a safe haven, a clean room and three meals a day. It was a new life, a total adventure full of education, laughs and learning some of life's most valuable lessons. I still refer to these lessons to this very day. I ain't going to college; I can't believe I used to repeat this over and over. Normally, if you repeat a phrase or saying over 21 times, it becomes habit and you begin to believe it. It then takes one person to positively reinforce and verbally tell you that you can, in fact, do it. Well fortunately for me my dad often was that one person, I could hear him from time to time saying "son college is important," don't ever forget that, son, you need to go college one day I promise you will love it! He was right. Whether it's two years, four years, private, public, HBCU or others, having a solid plan for your life after graduation is the most important thing. Educating yourself is a must. Your personal growth and development is the key to your own future. Once you get your degree life is not going to be handed to you on a silver platter just because you have achieved it. You can learn more about maximizing your college experience in my next book. I ain't going to college is no longer a part of my vocabulary and I hope it's no longer a part of yours either. No matter what you are going through, remember it's not where you start that matters but where you finish. Every day is a new day so start over tomorrow if you need to and write a new story in the book of life.

## *#Minutewithmarlo- Toolkit:*

## *Things to Remember*

Here are a few more things to consider as you prepare your plan for life after high school.

1.  College work is totally doable, but you have to study and put in the work.

2.  The better your grades are in high school the easier scholarships are to obtain, reducing the amount of money you will pay for school.

3. Join clubs that you like, not what your friends like

4. Study as much as possible for SAT/ACT. Downloading test prep apps and checking books out of the local library can help.

5. Get a mentor if you don't have one already

6. Pick a major that makes you happy and pays well

7. Don't say yes to any schools you have not visited in person

8. Volunteer often and log your hours

9. Have a top 10 prospective schools list. Then 5 then 3

10. Choose a school whether it's a two year or four year based on your personal goals and what you want to accomplish, not your friends or family member's goals. There is nothing wrong with getting input but chose wisely.

# Connect With Me Via Social Media!

Use the Hashtag *#minutewithmarlo* and tweet me your answers to any of the questions so that other people can share your point of view and we can all learn from each other. Use *#minutewithmarlo* to connect with me via Facebook or Instagram. Tag us in any pictures you take with the book and post your responses, and comments about the book!

Website: www.careerbounds.org

Facebook: www.Careerbounds/Facebook.com

Instagram: Careerbounds

Twitter: *Minutewithmarlo*

## Thank You

To my wonderful family Fonda, Reginald, and Lauren. Thank you for supporting me and allowing me to dedicate the proper time and effort to this project. I hope I can inspire others as much as you inspire me.

Made in the USA
Middletown, DE
07 January 2019